SCHOLASTIC

S0-BXP-568

Practice, Practice, Practice!

ADDITION & SUBTRACTION

by Betsy Franco

New York • Toronto • London • Auckland • Sydney
Mexico City • New Delhi • Hong Kong • Buenos Aires

Teaching
Resources

For Bessie,
who helped me practice

Scholastic Inc. grants teachers permission to photocopy the reproducible pages in this book for classroom use. No other part of this publication may be reproduced in whole or in part, or stored in a retrieval system, or transmitted in any form or by any means, electronic, mechanical, photocopying, recording, or otherwise, without written permission of the publisher. For information regarding permission, write to Scholastic Professional Books, 557 Broadway, New York, NY 10012.

Cover design by Maria Lilja

Cover and interior illustrations by Teresa Anderko

Interior design by Ellen Matlach for Boultinghouse & Boultinghouse, Inc.

ISBN: 0-439-57218-5

Contents

Addition

Subtraction

Addition & Subtraction

Introduction

Welcome to *Practice, Practice, Practice! Addition & Subtraction*. This book is packed with more than 50 reproducible activity sheets that give children practice in addition and subtraction skills, from basic facts to solving problems with three-digit numbers that require regrouping. The practice pages are flexible and easy to use—kids can complete them at home or in school, independently or in groups. Each activity features appealing illustrations, topics kids enjoy, and simple instructions so that children can work on their own. Pull out these practice pages for quick activities during the school day, or send them home as skill-building homework assignments.

The activities in *Practice, Practice, Practice! Addition & Subtraction* also coordinate with the standards recommended by the National Council of Teachers of Mathematics (NCTM). Some of the NCTM standards for content and processes covered in this book include numbers and operations; patterns, functions, and algebra; geometry and spatial sense; measurement; data analysis, statistics, and probability; problem solving; reasoning and proof; communication; connections; and representation.

These pages were designed to appeal to second and third graders. The topics relate to their world and interests: school, sports, pets, favorite foods, friends, shopping, and more! In addition, children will enjoy the variety of formats. They'll play a coin-toss game, shop at a pet store, balance animals on a scale, have a bobsled race, and much, much more. Many of the practice pages challenge children to go beyond solving addition and subtraction problems. For instance, in some of the activities, students will need to use their answers to create a number sequence, complete a crossword puzzle, and make comparisons. As further reinforcement, terms such as *equation, sum,* and *difference* are used throughout the book to help children become accustomed to reading and using the related math language.

For your convenience, a comprehensive answer key is included at the end of the book (pages 61–64). Each practice page is listed by title and page number. This easy reference will allow you or your students to check their completed pages for correct answers.

Whether you use the pages from *Practice, Practice, Practice! Addition & Subtraction* for homework or class work, they are sure to give your students an enjoyable way to get the extra practice and reinforcement they need to succeed in math!

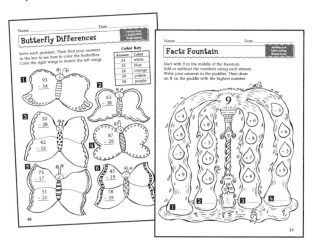

How to Use This Book

These practice pages were designed for flexible use. Children can work on them individually, in pairs, in small groups, or as a whole class. In addition, the ready-to-use pages provide ideal activities to leave for substitute teachers to use with the class. Have students work on the sheets:

- for reinforcement of basic addition and subtraction facts

- for review after a math unit is completed

- when they are finished with other class work

- as an activity to start or finish the day

- after lunch to settle back into learning

- as math center activities for practicing addition and subtraction facts

- as skill-building homework activities

Refer to the table of contents to locate the practice pages that address a particular type of addition or subtraction problem. For easy reference, the specific skills are also listed in a box near the top of each practice page. You can use the pages in the order they are presented or rearrange them to suit the needs of your students.

Most of the practice pages require only a pencil and eraser. A few require scissors, glue, and crayons. If sending home the sheets as homework, review the directions in advance to answer any questions that children have about the activity. You might also review the materials and modify them if necessary.

When children work on the practice pages independently, encourage them to read the directions and problems carefully before they begin to write on their pages. If desired, you may set up a buddy system, so that children can seek assistance from other classmates if the need arises.

If you plan to use the practice pages in a math center, be sure to place all the materials needed to complete the activities in the center. You may want to make a special folder for the activity pages for each addition and subtraction skill. Include a list of student names and a copy of the answer key for those pages in the folder, too. Then when children visit the center, they can work the assigned practice page, use the answer key to check their work, and check their names off the list to show that they finished the page.

Feel free to modify any of the practice pages to fit your students' specific needs. For example, you might replace the addend on each animal's body on page 8 (*Underwater Addition*) with any number, from 1 to 9, to create a practice page for different fact families. Encourage children to work together and share their problem-solving strategies as they work their way through the practice pages in this book.

Name _____ Date _____

Eight Chocolate Chips

Tanya ate two cookies at a time. Each pair of cookies had
8 chocolate chips. For each cookie pair below, draw a
different way that there can be 8 chocolate chips. Then
write an equation. The first one has been done for you.

1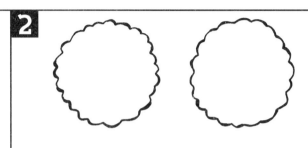

___1___ + ___7___ = ___8___

2

_____ + _____ = _____

3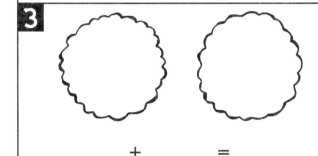

_____ + _____ = _____

4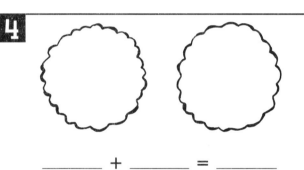

_____ + _____ = _____

5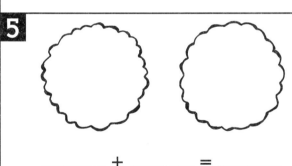

_____ + _____ = _____

6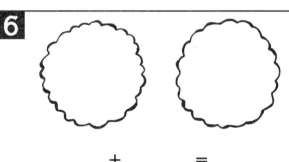

_____ + _____ = _____

7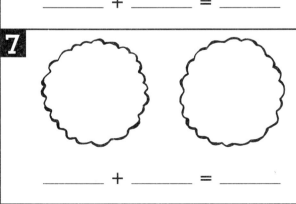

_____ + _____ = _____

8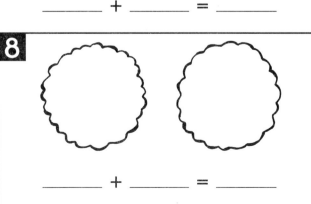

_____ + _____ = _____

Practice, Practice, Practice! Addition & Subtraction   Scholastic Teaching Resources

7

Underwater Addition

Add the numbers on each underwater animal to the number on its body. Write your answers in the circles. Use the back of the page to show how you got your answers.

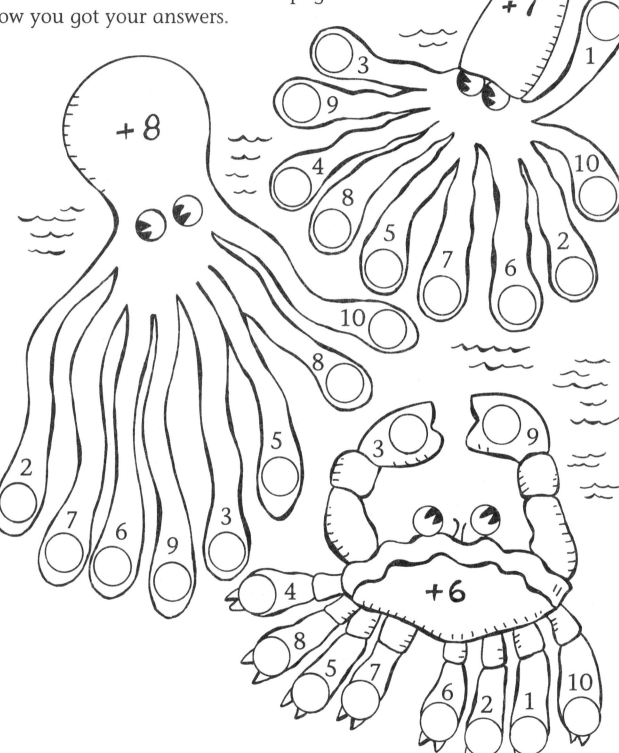

Practice, Practice, Practice! Addition & Subtraction   Scholastic Teaching Resources

Name _____ Date _____

Taking Inventory

It's time to take inventory at the department store.
Read each problem. Then write an equation to
answer the question. Use the back of the page to
show how you got your answers.

1 7 toy puppies
5 toy kittens

_____ + _____ = _____

How many toy animals
are in the store? _____

2 9 card games
6 board games

_____ + _____ = _____

How many games
are in the store? _____

3 7 ring floats
6 raft floats

_____ + _____ = _____

How many floats
are in the store? _____

4 7 chocolate candy bars
9 peanut candy bars

_____ + _____ = _____

How many candy
bars are in the store? _____

5  6 toy fire trucks
8 toy dump trucks

_____ + _____ = _____

How many toy trucks
are in the store? _____

6 10 wood chairs
10 metal chairs

_____ + _____ = _____

How many chairs
are in the store? _____

7 9 talking books
8 pop-up books

_____ + _____ = _____

How many books
are in the store? _____

8 4 large dog bowls
7 small dog bowls

_____ + _____ = _____

How many dog bowls
are in the store? _____

Puzzle Go-Togethers

Adding: Mixed Facts

To complete each equation, write the correct numbers in the puzzle pieces. Use only the numbers in the key. Hint: Each number can be used only one time.

KEY

5
6
7
8
9
10

A ⬚ + ⬚ = 18

B ⬚ + ⬚ = 11

C ⬚ + ⬚ = 16

KEY

4
5
6
9
11
13

D ⬚ + ⬚ = 19

E ⬚ + ⬚ = 16

F ⬚ + ⬚ = 13

Practice, Practice, Practice! Addition & Subtraction Scholastic Teaching Resources

Name _____ Date _____

Double Fun

Write an equation for each problem. Then find
the sum. The first one has been done for you.

1 How many
tails?

   __2__

   __1__ + __1__ = __2__

2 How many
tennis balls?

   _____

   ____ + ____ = ____

3 How many
wheels?

   _____

   ____ + ____ = ____

4 How many
toes?

   _____

   ____ + ____ = ____

5 How many
squares?

   _____

   ____ + ____ = ____

6 How many
spots?

   _____

   ____ + ____ = ____

7 How many
soccer players?

   _____

   ____ + ____ = ____

8 How many
eggs?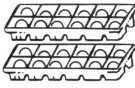

   _____

   ____ + ____ = ____

Draw a picture to match each equation. Then write the sum.

9 faces

   2 eyes + 2 eyes = _____ eyes

10 spiders

   8 legs + 8 legs = _____ legs

Practice, Practice, Practice! Addition & Subtraction Scholastic Teaching Resources

11

Name _____ Date _____

The Pet Store

Use the information from the sign to answer the questions. Write an equation for each problem. On the back of the page, show how you got your answers.

Pet Store

EACH MAMMAL #9
mouse, rabbit, hamster

EACH FISH #6
goldfish, angelfish, tetra

EACH REPTILE #7
snake, turtle, iguana

EACH AMPHIBIAN #8
toad, frog, salamander

1 Which two fish would you like to buy?

_____ and

_____

How much would they cost all together? $_____

$_____ + $_____ = $_____

2 Which two amphibians would you like to buy?

_____ and

_____

How much would they cost all together? $_____

$_____ + $_____ = $_____

3 Which two mammals would you like to buy?

_____ and

_____

How much would they cost all together? $_____

$_____ + $_____ = $_____

4 Which two reptiles would you like to buy?

_____ and

_____

How much would they cost all together? $_____

$_____ + $_____ = $_____

12

Practice, Practice, Practice! Addition & Subtraction   Scholastic Teaching Resources

Number Juggle

Help each clown find the missing number that
is needed to complete the equation. Write the
number on the ball. Use the back of the page
to show how you got your answers.

1 $7 + \underline{\quad} = 10$

2 $6 + \underline{\quad} = 13$

3 $9 + \underline{\quad} = 17$

4 $8 + \underline{\quad} = 12$

5 $9 + \underline{\quad} = 15$

6 $11 + \underline{\quad} = 13$

7 $10 + \underline{\quad} = 20$

8 $8 + \underline{\quad} = 13$

9 $7 + \underline{\quad} = 16$

10 Write the missing numbers in order from smallest to largest.

____ ____ ____ ____ ____ ____ ____ ____ ____

Three-Penny Pitch

Invite a friend to play this game with you. To play a round, take turns tossing three pennies onto the target. Use the numbers that you land on to write an addition problem on a sheet of paper. Then find the sum. The player with the higher score wins that round! Continue playing for 10 rounds.

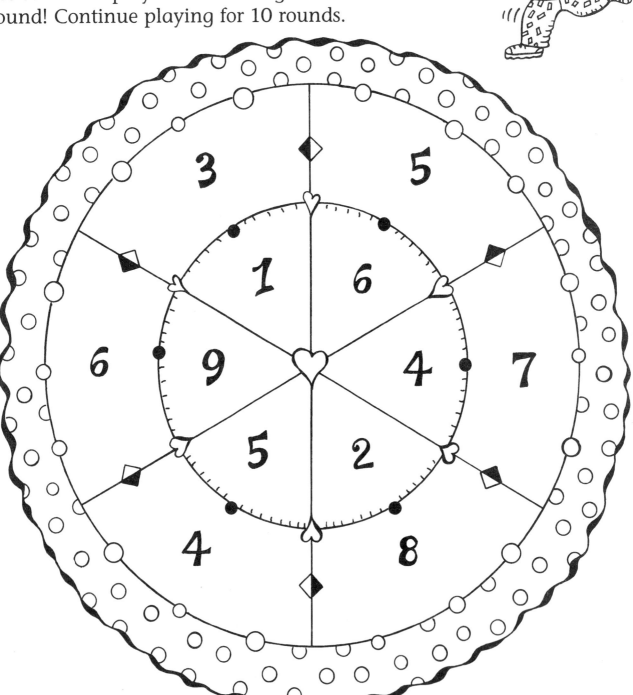

Practice, Practice, Practice! Addition & Subtraction Scholastic Teaching Resources

Balloon Tic-Tac-Toe

Look at the sum on each balloon stem. Then find three numbers in a row that can be added together to equal that sum. Draw a line through the numbers. Use the back of the page to show how you got your answers.

1

5	8	2
7	6	4
4	3	2

13

2

3	6	8
4	7	5
7	9	2

16

3

6	3	7
2	3	5
5	6	8

15

4

8	6	3
3	5	7
8	2	6

17

5

5	9	4
7	3	8
9	1	6

14

6

4	3	7
2	9	4
5	6	6

19

7

2	8	7
6	6	4
5	9	3

18

8

8	7	2
3	6	4
1	3	2

12

Practice, Practice, Practice! Addition & Subtraction Scholastic Teaching Resources

15

Billy's Baseball Caps

Look at the sum in the middle of each hat tree. Then help Billy fill in the numbers on his caps. He wants the three numbers on each side of the tree to add up to the sum in the middle. Use only the numbers in the key. For each tree, the numbers on two caps have already been filled in. Hint: A number cannot be used more than once on each tree.

KEY
1 2 3
4 5 6

Practice, Practice, Practice! Addition & Subtraction Scholastic Teaching Resources

Scoring Goals

Look at the sum on each soccer ball. Find the two
numbers on the goal that can be added together
to equal that sum. Use the back of the page to show
how you got your answers. Then draw a line through
the two numbers. Score!

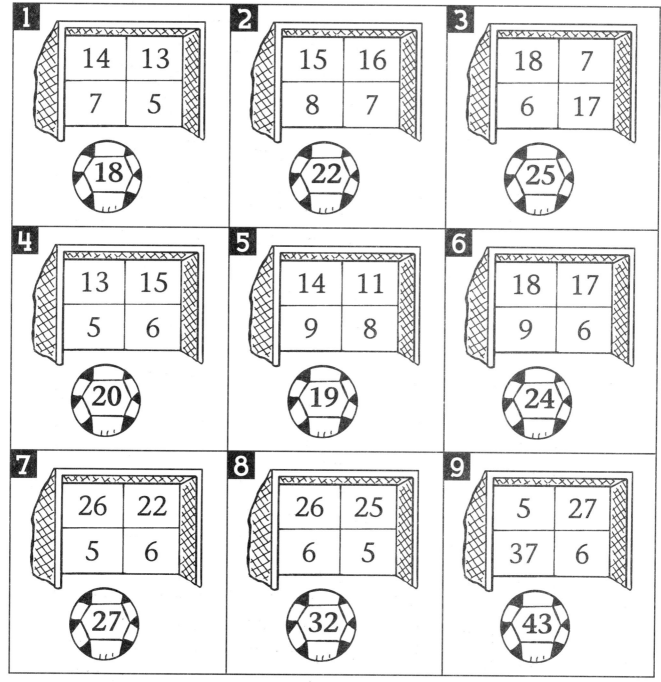

1

14	13
7	5

18

2

15	16
8	7

22

3

18	7
6	17

25

4

13	15
5	6

20

5

14	11
9	8

19

6

18	17
9	6

24

7

26	22
5	6

27

8

26	25
6	5

32

9

5	27
37	6

43

Little Pig's Problem

Little Pig has a big problem! His homework got crushed in his book bag, and now he can't read it. To help Little Pig fix his homework, find each missing number. Then write the number in the box. Use the back of the page to show how you got your answers.

1
$$
\begin{array}{r}
4\,7 \\
+\ \ 6 \\
\hline
5\ \square
\end{array}
$$

2
$$
\begin{array}{r}
3\ \square \\
+\,4\,3 \\
\hline
7\,8
\end{array}
$$

3
$$
\begin{array}{r}
2\,8 \\
+\,1\ \square \\
\hline
4\,2
\end{array}
$$

4
$$
\begin{array}{r}
\square\,4 \\
+\,3\ \square \\
\hline
8\,8
\end{array}
$$

5
$$
\begin{array}{r}
8\,5 \\
+\ \ \square \\
\hline
9\,1
\end{array}
$$

6
$$
\begin{array}{r}
\square\ \square \\
+\,3\,4 \\
\hline
5\,7
\end{array}
$$

7
$$
\begin{array}{r}
1\ \square \\
+\,\square\,6 \\
\hline
8\,9
\end{array}
$$

8
$$
\begin{array}{r}
6\,9 \\
+\,2\ \square \\
\hline
\square\,7
\end{array}
$$

9
$$
\begin{array}{r}
\square\,2 \\
+\,2\ \square \\
\hline
7\,8
\end{array}
$$

Practice, Practice, Practice! Addition & Subtraction Scholastic Teaching Resources

Name _____ Date _____

Amazing Adding Machines

Each of Amanda's machines adds the number put into it to the number shown on the machine. To show how each machine works, fill in the number on the blank ball. Then write an equation. The first one has been done for you.

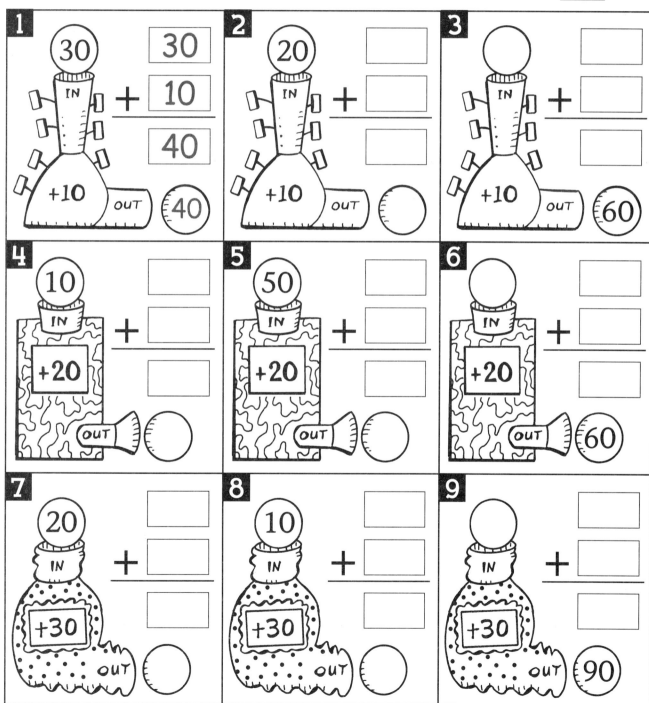

1 30 IN +10 OUT 40

$$30 + 10 \over 40$$

2 20 IN +10 OUT ◯

$$+$$

3 ◯ IN +10 OUT 60

$$+$$

4 10 IN +20 OUT ◯

$$+$$

5 50 IN +20 OUT ◯

$$+$$

6 ◯ IN +20 OUT 60

$$+$$

7 20 IN +30 OUT ◯

$$+$$

8 10 IN +30 OUT ◯

$$+$$

9 ◯ IN +30 OUT 90

$$+$$

Practice, Practice, Practice! Addition & Subtraction Scholastic Teaching Resources

19

Flower-Box Sums

Adding:
2 Digits Without
Regrouping

Look at the sum on each flower. Then find two bricks in a row that have numbers on them that can be added together to equal that sum. Draw a circle around the two numbers. The first one has been done for you. Hint: Numbers can be added across, down, or diagonally.

| 56 | 59 | 65 | 68 | 76 | 79 | 83 | 87 | 97 | 98 |

14	67	41	44	37
42	11	31	43	47
29	59	21	15	38
31	43	33	62	24
34	10	12	55	23
36	61	45	37	22
25	55	23	67	21

20

Practice, Practice, Practice! Addition & Subtraction Scholastic Teaching Resources

Name _____ Date _____

Easy-Add Estimates

Try this trick to estimate sums to addition problems. First, round each number up or down to the nearest 10. Use your rounded numbers to write a new problem. Then find the sum to both problems. The first one has been done for you.

Example:

27	Round 27 up to 30.	30
+ 42	Round 42 down to 40.	+ 40
69	The actual sum should be close to 70.	70

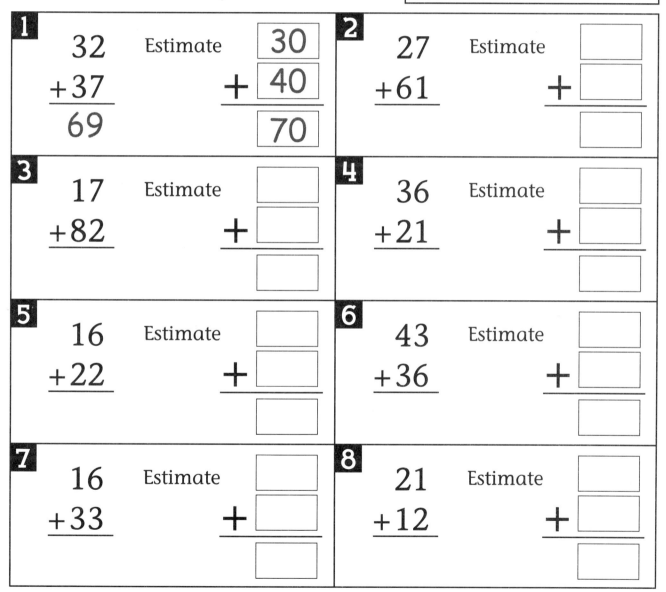

1
```
  32    Estimate    30
+37               +  40
─────             ─────
  69                70
```

2
```
  27    Estimate    ☐
+61               + ☐
                    ☐
```

3
```
  17    Estimate    ☐
+82               + ☐
                    ☐
```

4
```
  36    Estimate    ☐
+21               + ☐
                    ☐
```

5
```
  16    Estimate    ☐
+22               + ☐
                    ☐
```

6
```
  43    Estimate    ☐
+36               + ☐
                    ☐
```

7
```
  16    Estimate    ☐
+33               + ☐
                    ☐
```

8
```
  21    Estimate    ☐
+12               + ☐
                    ☐
```

9 To make a number pattern, write your estimated sums in order from smallest to largest.

____ ____ ____ ____ ____ ____ ____ ____

Playful Pup

Adding:
2 Digits With
Regrouping

Poor Davy! Playful Pup ripped up his addition homework. To help Davy put his problems back together, find the sum for each equation. Then draw a line to the torn piece of paper that has the matching sum. Use the back of the page to show how you got your answers.

1
$$45$$
$$+17$$

2
$$53$$
$$+29$$

3
$$26$$
$$+25$$

4
$$37$$
$$+47$$

5
$$38$$
$$+16$$

6
$$78$$
$$+18$$

7
$$69$$
$$+28$$

97

82

84

96

62

54

51

22

Practice, Practice, Practice! Addition & Subtraction Scholastic Teaching Resources

Name _____ Date _____

Animal Mail

Paul Possum delivers all the mail from the Muddy Pond Post Office. Write an equation to show how far Paul must travel to deliver each letter.

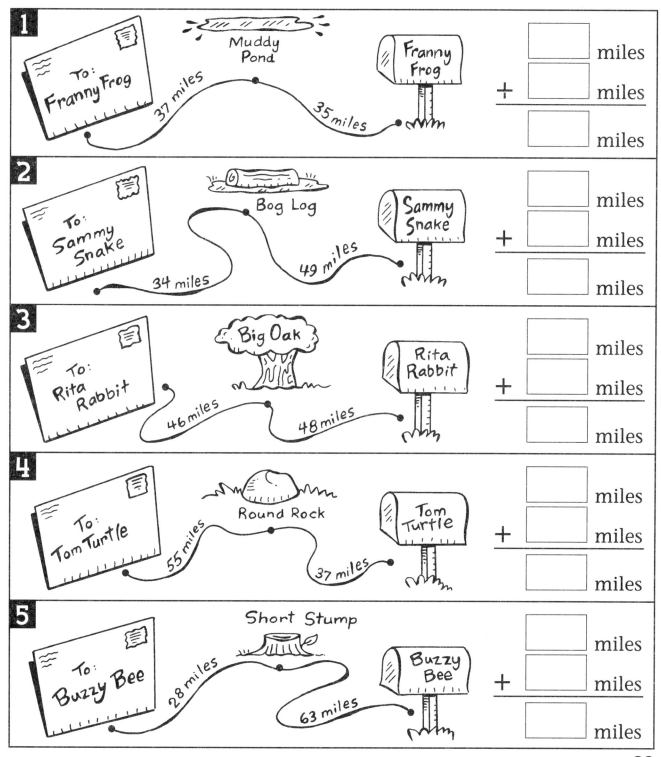

1. To: Franny Frog — Muddy Pond — 37 miles — 35 miles — Franny Frog
   ☐ miles + ☐ miles = ☐ miles

2. To: Sammy Snake — Bog Log — 34 miles — 49 miles — Sammy Snake
   ☐ miles + ☐ miles = ☐ miles

3. To: Rita Rabbit — Big Oak — 46 miles — 48 miles — Rita Rabbit
   ☐ miles + ☐ miles = ☐ miles

4. To: Tom Turtle — Round Rock — 55 miles — 37 miles — Tom Turtle
   ☐ miles + ☐ miles = ☐ miles

5. To: Buzzy Bee — Short Stump — 28 miles — 63 miles — Buzzy Bee
   ☐ miles + ☐ miles = ☐ miles

Practice, Practice, Practice! Addition & Subtraction   Scholastic Teaching Resources

23

Name _____ Date _____

Sum Challenge

5   6   7   8

1

Use the numbers above to write an equation with the largest possible sum.

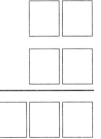

Now use the numbers to write another equation that has the same sum.

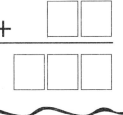

2

Use the numbers above to write an equation with the smallest possible sum.

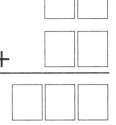

Now use the numbers to write another equation that has the same sum.

6   7   8   9

3

Use the numbers above to write an equation with the largest possible sum.

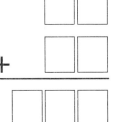

Now use the numbers to write another equation that has the same sum.

4

Use the numbers above to write an equation with the smallest possible sum.

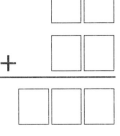

Now use the numbers to write another equation that has the same sum.

Name _____ Date _____

Silly Sal

Silly Sal just finished her math problems. To check her work, write and solve each problem next to Sal's completed problem. If Sal's sum matches your sum, mark the "correct" box. If the sums do not match, check your work again. If your sum stays the same, mark Sal's problem "incorrect." The first one has been done for you.

1
```
  47      47
+ 64    + 64
 111     111
```
☑ correct
☐ incorrect

2
```
  23
+ 98
 113
```
☐ correct
☐ incorrect

3
```
  66
+ 86
 152
```
☐ correct
☐ incorrect

4
```
  99
+ 79
 178
```
☐ correct
☐ incorrect

5
```
  57
+ 57
 124
```
☐ correct
☐ incorrect

6
```
  89
+ 96
 185
```
☐ correct
☐ incorrect

7
```
  78
+ 48
 136
```
☐ correct
☐ incorrect

8
```
  87
+ 56
 143
```
☐ correct
☐ incorrect

9
```
  88
+ 88
 174
```
☐ correct
☐ incorrect

Practice, Practice, Practice! Addition & Subtraction Scholastic Teaching Resources

25

Name _____ Date _____

On the Road

Tom took four road trips last year. To find out how far Tom traveled, read each problem. Then use the map to find the distance in kilometers (km) between the places. Write an equation and solve it.

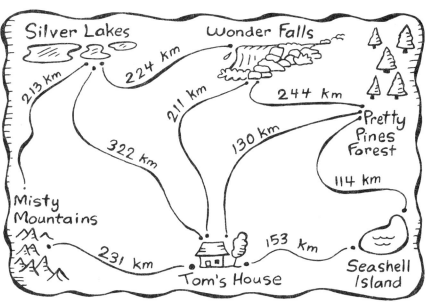

Silver Lakes   Wonder Falls

213 km   224 km

211 km   244 km

322 km   130 km   Pretty Pines Forest

114 km

Misty Mountains

231 km   153 km

Tom's House   Seashell Island

---

1 Tom left his house to visit Silver Lakes and Wonder Falls. Then he went home. How far did he travel?

☐ km
☐ km
+ ☐ km
————
☐ km

_____ km

---

2 Tom left his house to visit Wonder Falls and Pretty Pines Forest. Then he went home. How far did he travel?

☐ km
☐ km
+ ☐ km
————
☐ km

_____ km

---

3 Tom left his house to visit Misty Mountains and Silver Lakes. Then he went home. How far did he travel?

☐ km
☐ km
+ ☐ km
————
☐ km

_____ km

---

4 Tom left his house to visit Pretty Pines Forest and Seashell Island. Then he went home. How far did he travel?

☐ km
☐ km
+ ☐ km
————
☐ km

_____ km

Practice, Practice, Practice! Addition & Subtraction Scholastic Teaching Resources

Name _____ Date _____

Balancing Animals

Cut out the animals at the bottom of the page. Glue two more animals on each scale to balance it. Write an equation.

A short way to write **pounds** is **lb.**

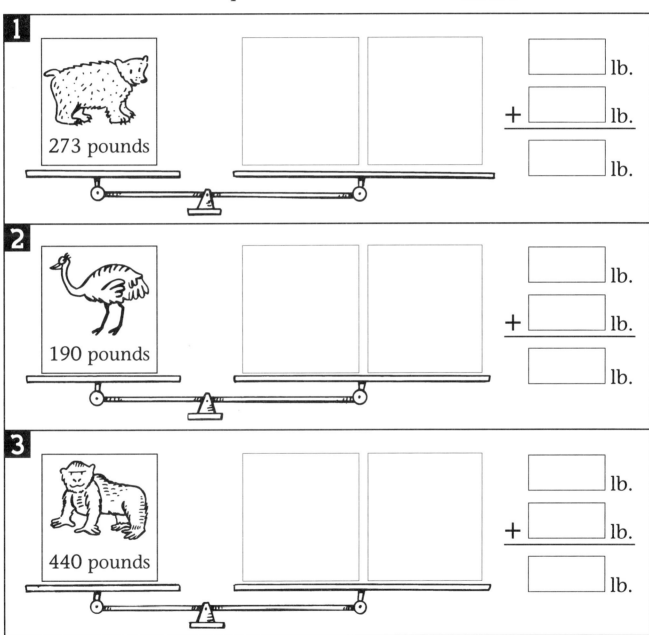

1

273 pounds

☐ lb.
+ ☐ lb.
———
☐ lb.

2

190 pounds

☐ lb.
+ ☐ lb.
———
☐ lb.

3

440 pounds

☐ lb.
+ ☐ lb.
———
☐ lb.

 135 pounds  356 pounds  84 pounds 55 pounds  206 pounds 67 pounds

Name _____ Date _____

Twins Buy Bikes

Rhonda and Roger Raccoon went to the bike store to buy the things they needed for the big bike race. At the checkout stand, the two raccoons learned that they had picked out all the same things! Look at how much each item costs. Then write an equation to show how much the raccoons spent all together.

1 How much did they spend for two helmets?

$ _____

2 How much did they spend for two bike pumps?

$ _____

3 How much did they spend for two bike locks?

$ _____

4 How much did they spend for two pairs of biking shoes?

$ _____

5 How much did they spend for two sets of biking clothes?

$ _____

6 How much did they spend for two bikes?

$ _____

Practice, Practice, Practice! Addition & Subtraction Scholastic Teaching Resources

Name _____ Date _____

Big Creature Comparisons

Read each problem. Use the information from the key to find out how tall each creature is. Then write an equation.

Creature Height Key

Hippoboa 187 feet

Googlepup 368 feet

Reptilio 235 feet

Monsterdon 566 feet

Bigfooter 299 feet

Robotosaur 474 feet

---

1 Which creature is 175 feet taller than Bigfooter?

☐ feet
+ ☐ feet
_____
☐ feet

2 Which creature is 379 feet taller than Hippoboa?

☐ feet
+ ☐ feet
_____
☐ feet

---

3 Which creature is 133 feet taller than Reptilio?

☐ feet
+ ☐ feet
_____
☐ feet

4 Which creature is 181 feet taller than Hippoboa?

☐ feet
+ ☐ feet
_____
☐ feet

---

5 Which creature is 198 feet taller than Googlepup?

☐ feet
+ ☐ feet
_____
☐ feet

6 Which creature is 106 feet taller than Googlepup?

☐ feet
+ ☐ feet
_____
☐ feet

Practice, Practice, Practice! Addition & Subtraction   Scholastic Teaching Resources

29

Name _____ Date _____

Box of Chocolates

Cindy Chipmunk had 10 chocolates in each box of candy. She opened the boxes to taste the chocolates inside. Look at how many chocolates are in each box now. Then answer the question. Write an equation to show how you got your answer. The first one has been done for you.

1

$$10 - 3 = 7$$

How many chocolates did Cindy eat? ___7___

2

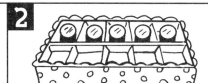

How many chocolates did Cindy eat? _____

3

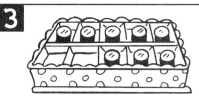

How many chocolates did Cindy eat? _____

4

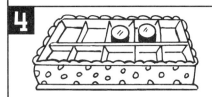

How many chocolates did Cindy eat? _____

5

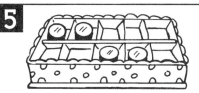

How many chocolates did Cindy eat? _____

6

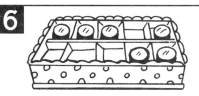

How many chocolates did Cindy eat? _____

7

How many chocolates did Cindy eat? _____

8

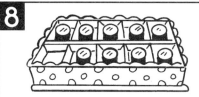

How many chocolates did Cindy eat? _____

9

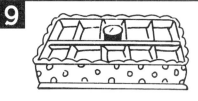

How many chocolates did Cindy eat? _____

Practice, Practice, Practice! Addition & Subtraction   Scholastic Teaching Resources

Bobsled Race

Ask a friend to keep track of your time with a stopwatch when you play this game. First, cut out the game cards on page 32. Then place 10 cards faceup on the game board.

To play, find the differences on the game cards as fast as you can. Be sure to begin at Start and end at Finish. Write down your time. Then invite your friend to take a turn. Challenge: Put different cards on the game board and then take another turn. Can you beat your first time?

Bobsled Race Game Cards

5 – 3	14 – 5	6 – 4	12 – 4	9 – 3
13 – 6	16 – 7	13 – 8	11 – 5	10 – 3
8 – 4	15 – 7	17 – 8	10 – 7	7 – 3
11 – 7	9 – 5	14 – 8	9 – 7	11 – 6
12 – 5	10 – 6	18 – 9	15 – 9	8 – 3
14 – 7	14 – 9	12 – 6	8 – 5	17 – 9
13 – 9	16 – 8	15 – 6	10 – 5	7 – 2
14 – 6	11 – 4	12 – 7	8 – 6	9 – 8

Name _____   Date _____

Free Mr. Fly

Miss Spider will set Mr. Fly free after all the problems in her web have been solved. To help Mr. Fly get free, solve each subtraction problem. Write the difference on the web. Then check the key for the matching number. If each number in the key matches one of your answers, then you subtracted correctly. Mr. Fly can go free!

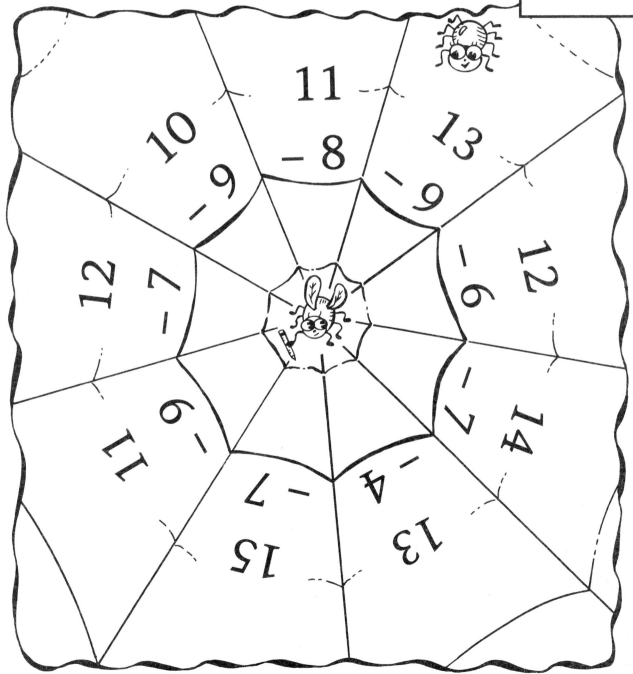

Practice, Practice, Practice! Addition & Subtraction   Scholastic Teaching Resources

33

Name _____ Date _____

Animal Tracks

For each problem, write an equation on the line to show how to find the difference. Then answer the question.

1

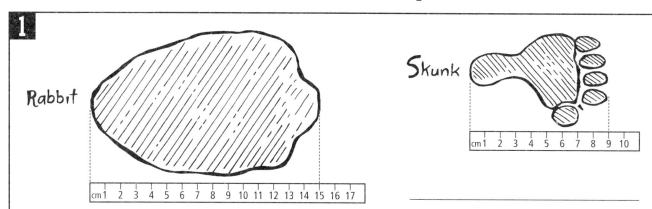

How much longer is the rabbit track? _____ cm

2

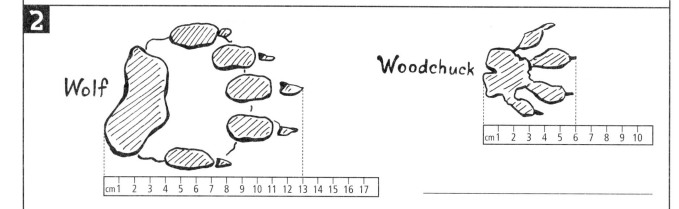

How much longer is the wolf track? _____ cm

3

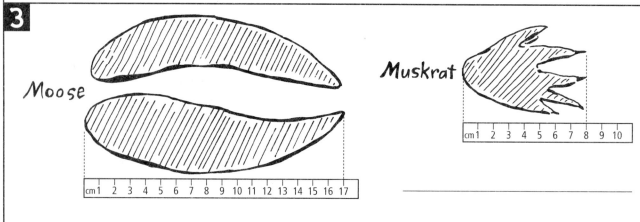

How much longer is the moose track? _____ cm

34

Name _____   Date _____

Jungle Trail

Invite a few friends to play this game with you. Place a game marker on Start for each player. Take turns rolling a number cube to see how many spaces to move. Move that many spaces. Then find the difference for the problem on that space. If your answer is correct, leave the marker on the space. If it is not correct, move the marker back to Start. The first player to reach Finish is the winner!

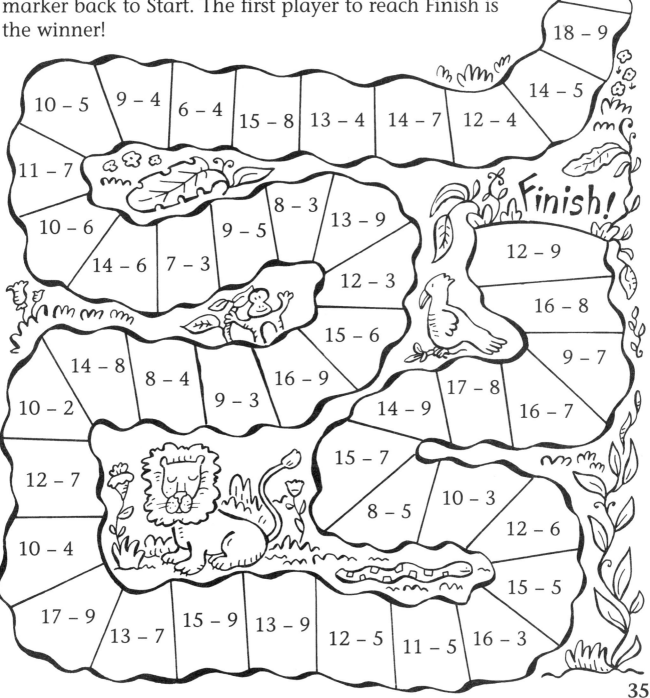

Name _____ Date _____

Bug Olympics

Six bugs raced in the Marathon Mile during the Bug Olympics. Look at the chart to see how long each bug took to finish the race. Then use the information to answer each question. Write an equation to show how you got your answer.

Marathon Mile Results	
Bug	Time to Finish
Snail	16 hours
caterpillar	9 hours
roly-poly	12 hours
beetle	8 hours
ant	7 hours
slug	18 hours

1 How much longer did the snail take than the beetle?

_____ hours

_____

2 How much longer did the roly-poly take than the ant?

_____ hours

_____

3 Which bug took 9 hours less than the slug?

the _____

_____

4 Which bug took 4 hours less than the snail?

the _____

_____

5 How much less time did the caterpillar take than the roly-poly bug?

_____ hours

_____

6 How much longer did the slowest bug take than the fastest bug?

_____ hours

_____

36

Practice, Practice, Practice! Addition & Subtraction Scholastic Teaching Resources

People and Pets

For each problem, find the difference between the age of the pet and its owner. Write an equation to show how you got your answer.

1

56 years   4 years   □ − □
                        □

Sam is _____ years older than his dog.

2

28 years   3 years   □ − □
                        □

Tina is _____ years older than her mouse.

3

6 years   89 years   □ − □
                        □

Joe's turtle is _____ years older than Joe.

4

74 years   2 years   □ − □
                        □

Nana is _____ years older than her bird.

5

4 years   15 years   □ − □
                        □

Tara's cat is _____ years older than Tara.

6

47 years   3 years   □ − □
                        □

Nick is _____ years older than his horse.

7

68 years   5 years   □ − □
                        □

Cally is _____ years older than her snake.

8

8 years   29 years   □ − □
                        □

Ben's iguana is _____ years older than Ben.

Practice, Practice, Practice! Addition & Subtraction Scholastic Teaching Resources

37

Bunny Board Toss

Invite a friend to play this game with you. You will need this score sheet, the game board on page 39, and a number cube.

To play a round, each player tosses the number cube onto the game board. Then the player subtracts the number on the cube from the number that the cube lands on. The player writes an equation for the problem on his or her side of the score sheet. To find out who won the round, circle the problem with the higher answer. Continue playing for 10 rounds.

Score Sheet

Round	Player 1	Player 2
1		
2		
3		
4		
5		
6		
7		
8		
9		
10		

Practice, Practice, Practice! Addition & Subtraction Scholastic Teaching Resources

Bunny Board Toss Game Board

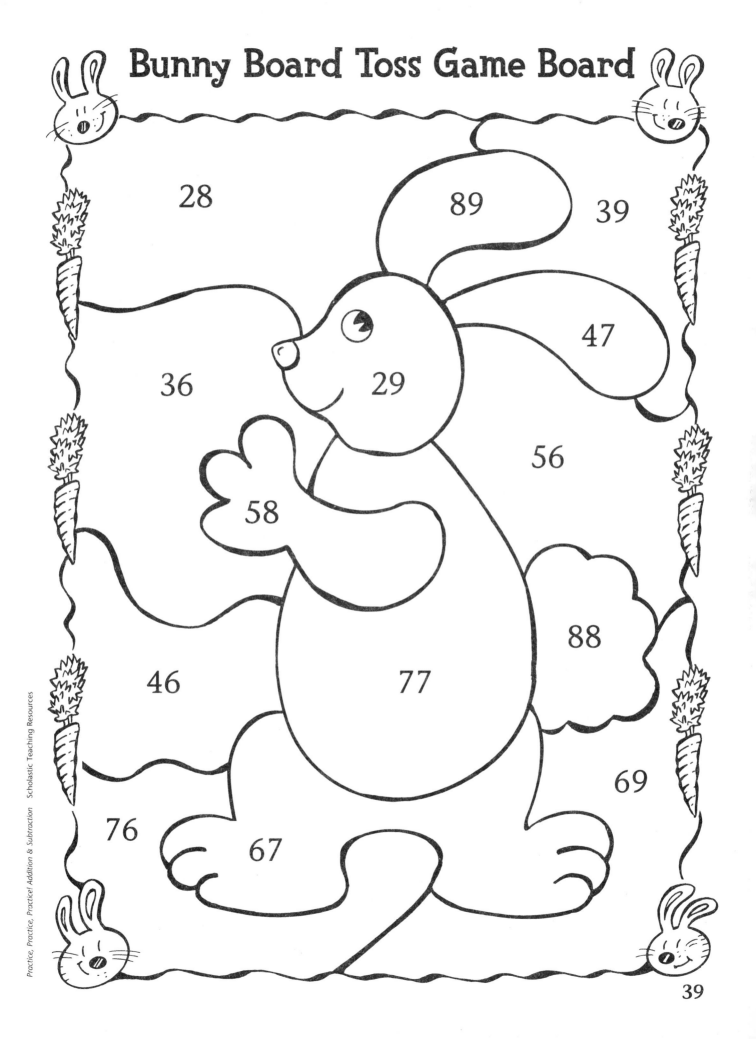

28
89
39
47
36
29
56
58
46
77
88
76
67
69

Name _____ Date _____

Four From Three

Use these numbers to make four different subtraction problems: **3 2 5**

Solve each problem.

 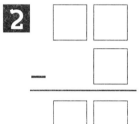 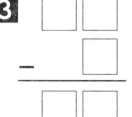 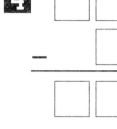

Use these numbers to make four different subtraction problems: **4 5 6**

Solve each problem.

 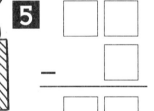 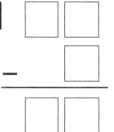 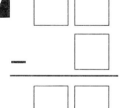 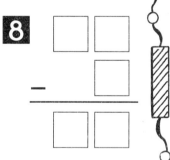

Practice, Practice, Practice! Addition & Subtraction Scholastic Teaching Resources

Name _____   Date _____

Giant-Size Subtraction

Limburger is a bigger giant than Bree.
For each problem, find the difference in
centimeters (cm) between the two giants'
sizes. Then write your answer on the line.
Use the back of the page to show how
you got your answers.

1 Limburger's
waist size is 232
cm. Bree's waist
is 9 cm smaller.
What is Bree's
waist size?

☐ cm
− ☐ cm
☐ cm

_____ cm

2 Limburger's
foot is 153 cm
long. Bree's foot
is 6 cm shorter.
How long is
Bree's foot?

☐ cm
− ☐ cm
☐ cm

_____ cm

3 Limburger's
chest size is
191 cm. Bree's
chest is 8 cm
smaller. What is
Bree's chest size?

☐ cm
− ☐ cm
☐ cm

_____ cm

4 Limburger's
arm is 134 cm
long. Bree's arm
is 7 cm shorter.
How long is
Bree's arm?

☐ cm
− ☐ cm
☐ cm

_____ cm

5 Limburger's
leg is 248 cm
long. Bree's leg
is 9 cm shorter.
How long is
Bree's leg?

☐ cm
− ☐ cm
☐ cm

_____ cm

6 Limburger
is 386 cm tall.
Bree is 7 cm
shorter. How
tall is Bree?

☐ cm
− ☐ cm
☐ cm

_____ cm

Challenge!

Invite a friend to play this game with you. First, cut out the cards on this page and page 43. Then divide them evenly between the players, keeping the cards facedown.

To play, each player turns over the top card on his or her stack of cards and then solves the problem. The player with the card that has the larger answer wins the round. If the answer on both cards is the same, players slip their own cards back into the playing stack. Continue playing until all the cards have been used.

60 −10	50 −30	80 −30	40 −10
20 −10	40 −20	90 −60	90 −50
60 −50	60 −20	50 −20	80 −60

Practice, Practice, Practice! Addition & Subtraction Scholastic Teaching Resources

Challenge! Game Cards

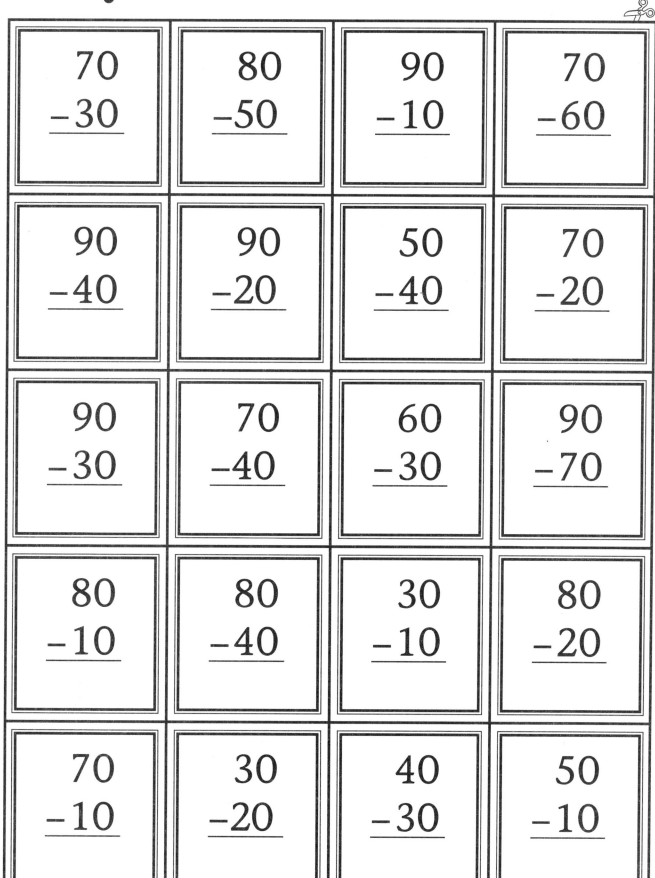

70 −30	80 −50	90 −10	70 −60
90 −40	90 −20	50 −40	70 −20
90 −30	70 −40	60 −30	90 −70
80 −10	80 −40	30 −10	80 −20
70 −10	30 −20	40 −30	50 −10

Practice, Practice, Practice! Addition & Subtraction   Scholastic Teaching Resources

43

Name _____   Date _____

Space Subtraction

Solve the problem in each spaceship. Then draw a line
from the spaceship to the alien with the matching
answer. Color the alien and the spaceship the same color.

1
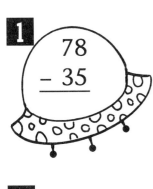
$$\begin{array}{r} 78 \\ -\ 35 \\ \hline \end{array}$$

2
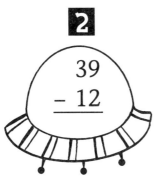
$$\begin{array}{r} 39 \\ -\ 12 \\ \hline \end{array}$$

3
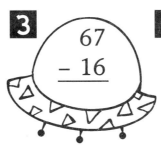
$$\begin{array}{r} 67 \\ -\ 16 \\ \hline \end{array}$$

4
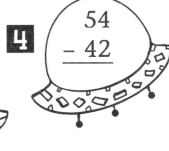
$$\begin{array}{r} 54 \\ -\ 42 \\ \hline \end{array}$$

5
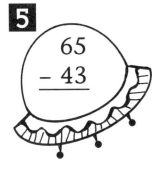
$$\begin{array}{r} 65 \\ -\ 43 \\ \hline \end{array}$$

6
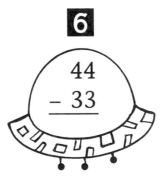
$$\begin{array}{r} 44 \\ -\ 33 \\ \hline \end{array}$$

7

$$\begin{array}{r} 86 \\ -\ 52 \\ \hline \end{array}$$

8
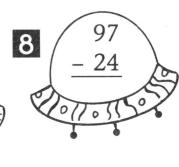
$$\begin{array}{r} 97 \\ -\ 24 \\ \hline \end{array}$$

73

11

22

27

51

12

43

34

44

Practice, Practice, Practice! Addition & Subtraction   Scholastic Teaching Resources

Subtraction Shape Sentences

Subtracting: 2 Digits Without Regrouping

Fill in the blank shape to complete each subtraction problem. Use the back of the page to show how you got your answers.

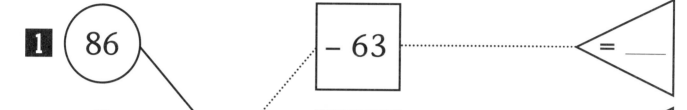

1 86   – 63   = ____

2 47   – ____   = 23

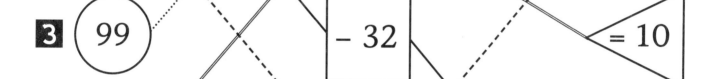

3 99   – 32   = 10

4 25   – ____   = ____

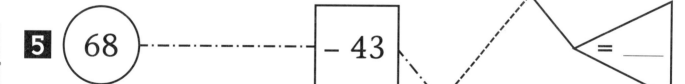

5 68   – 43   = ____

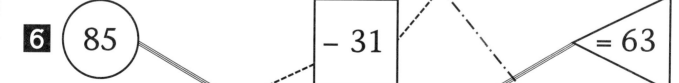

6 85   – 31   = 63

7 79   – ____   = ____

Practice, Practice, Practice! Addition & Subtraction   Scholastic Teaching Resources

45

Name _____ Date _____

How Late Is Sam?

Subtracting: 2 Digits Without Regrouping

Sam Squirrel is late for everything! Look at each sign. Then read the problem. Write an equation using only the minutes to show how late Sam is. Write your answer on the line.

1

Acorn Hunt
★ ★ ★ ★ ★
September 14
6:30 A.M.

Sam arrives at 6:42 A.M.

$$\begin{array}{r} 42 \\ -\ 30 \\ \hline \end{array}$$

Sam is _____ minutes late.

2

🍂 FALL 🍂
Good-bye Party
October 23
5:25 P.M.

Sam scurries in at 5:57 P.M.

Sam is _____ minutes late.

3

Hello, Spring Party
April 12
1:15 P.M.

Sam comes at 1:28 P.M.

Sam is _____ minutes late.

4

S quirrel
Y oga
May 5
8:45 A.M.

Sam drops in at 8:56 A.M.

Sam is _____ minutes late.

5

Tree Race
June 5
3:26 P.M.

Sam races in at 3:49 P.M.

Sam is _____ minutes late.

6

Squirrel Olympics
August 15
4:35 A.M.

Sam jogs in at 4:58 A.M.

Sam is _____ minutes late.

46

Name _____ Date _____

The Pond Store

Use the information from the sign to solve each problem. Write an equation to show how you got your answer. Then write your answer on the line. The first one has been done for you.

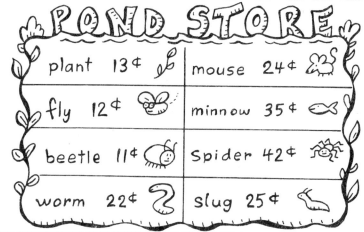

POND STORE

plant 13¢	mouse 24¢
fly 12¢	minnow 35¢
beetle 11¢	spider 42¢
worm 22¢	slug 25¢

1 Snake has 68¢. How much will she have left if she buys:

a mouse? ___44___ ¢

$$\begin{array}{r} 68¢ \\ -24¢ \\ \hline 44¢ \end{array}$$

a minnow? _____ ¢

a slug? _____ ¢

2 Lizard has 89¢. How much will he have left if he buys:

a plant? _____ ¢

a fly? _____ ¢

a spider? _____ ¢

3 Turtle has 46¢. How much will she have left if she buys:

a minnow? _____ ¢

a plant? _____ ¢

a worm? _____ ¢

4 Frog has 57¢. How much will he have left if he buys:

a fly? _____ ¢

a worm? _____ ¢

a beetle? _____ ¢

Practice, Practice, Practice! Addition & Subtraction Scholastic Teaching Resources

47

Name _____ Date _____

Butterfly Differences

Solve each problem. Then find your answers in the key to see how to color the butterflies. Color the right wings to match the left wings.

Color Key

Answer	Color
24	white
25	blue
26	orange
39	yellow
58	purple

1

$$93 - 54$$

2

$$63 - 38$$

3

$$52 - 28$$

$$42 - 16$$

4

$$87 - 29$$

5

$$75 - 17$$

$$51 - 25$$

6

$$45 - 19$$

$$78 - 39$$

Practice, Practice, Practice! Addition & Subtraction Scholastic Teaching Resources

Name _____ Date _____

Checking Chuck

Chuck kept falling asleep while doing his homework. Check each of Chuck's subtraction answers by using addition. If his answer is correct, draw a ✔ next to it. If it is not correct, draw an **X** through it. Then correct the problem. The first one has been done for you. Hint: Chuck's problem will be correct if the top number in his problem matches the sum of your addition problem.

1 Chuck's subtraction:
$$65 - 26 = \boxed{39} \checkmark$$
Check Chuck:
$$26 + 39 = \boxed{65}$$
Correct if needed:
$$65 - 26 = \boxed{}$$

2 Chuck's subtraction:
$$41 - 25 = \boxed{17}$$
Check Chuck:
$$\boxed{25} + 17 = \boxed{}$$
Correct if needed:
$$41 - 25 = \boxed{}$$

3 Chuck's subtraction:
$$83 - 65 = \boxed{28}$$
Check Chuck:
$$\boxed{} + 28 = \boxed{}$$
Correct if needed:
$$83 - 65 = \boxed{}$$

4 Chuck's subtraction:
$$54 - 28 = \boxed{24}$$
Check Chuck:
$$\boxed{} + \boxed{} = \boxed{}$$
Correct if needed:
$$54 - 28 = \boxed{}$$

5 Chuck's subtraction:
$$92 - 57 = \boxed{35}$$
Check Chuck:
$$\boxed{} + \boxed{} = \boxed{}$$
Correct if needed:
$$92 - 57 = \boxed{}$$

Number Connection

To complete this puzzle, solve the
subtraction problems on page 51.
Then write each answer in the puzzle.

Name _____ Date _____

Number Connection Clues

Solve each subtraction problem. Then write the answer in the puzzle on page 50. On the back of the page, show how your got your answers.

Across

A. 32
− 18

D. 91
− 15

F. 90
− 18

H. 67
− 19

I. 53
− 28

J. 62
− 25

K. 72
− 18

M. 65
− 19

N. 91
− 28

O. 76
− 38

P. 96
− 49

Down

B. 83
− 36

C. 94
− 17

E. 93
− 29

G. 76
− 48

I. 52
− 26

J. 83
− 49

L. 64
− 18

O. 55
− 18

P. 72
− 29

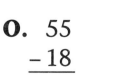

Practice, Practice, Practice! Addition & Subtraction Scholastic Teaching Resources

51

Name _____ Date _____

Magazine Subtraction

Make up your own fun subtraction problems. First, cut out 2-digit numbers from magazines or newspapers. Glue a number to each gray box. Be sure to glue the larger number to the top box in each problem. Then subtract to find the difference. Write your answer on the line.

1 Number of Tim's brothers **17**

Number of Tim's sisters **– 11**

6

Tim has __6__ more brothers than sisters.

2 Number of hot dogs James ate

Number of hamburgers Sam ate **–**

James ate _____ more hot dogs than hamburgers.

3 Number of Jen's rabbits

Number of Jen's cats **–**

Jen has _____ more rabbits than cats.

4 Number of Sue's e-mails

Number of Sue's voice mails **–**

Sue has _____ more e-mails than voice mails.

5 Number of Bo's chocolates

Number of Bo's lollipops **–**

Bo has _____ more chocolates than lollipops.

6 Hockey goals Maria scored

Soccer goals Maria scored **–**

Maria scored _____ more goals in hockey than in soccer.

Practice, Practice, Practice! Addition & Subtraction Scholastic Teaching Resources

Name _____   Date _____

Collection Kids

Read each problem. Subtract to find the difference. Then write your answer on the line. Use the back of the page to show how you got your answers.

1 Kevin and Meg have 700 bottle caps all together. Kevin has 500 bottle caps. How many bottle caps does Meg have?

_____ bottle caps

2 Nina and Jim have 900 ants all together in their ant farms. Nina has 600 ants. How many ants does Jim have?

_____ ants

3 Don and Maya have 600 baseball cards all together. Don has 100 baseball cards. How many baseball cards does Maya have?

_____ baseball cards

4 Muhammed and Karen have 900 paper clips all together. Muhammed has 200 paper clips. How many paper clips does Karen have?

_____ paper clips

5 Michiko and Greg have 400 stamps all together. Michiko has 100 stamps. How many stamps does Greg have?

_____ stamps

6 Peter and Jada have 700 marbles all together. Peter has 300 marbles. How many marbles does Jada have?

_____ marbles

7 Tonia and Mike have 800 stickers all together. Tonia has 400 stickers. How many stickers does Mike have?

_____ stickers

8 Brian and Sumi have 600 pennies all together. Brian has 200 pennies. How many pennies does Sumi have?

_____ pennies

Name _____ Date _____

Basketball Scores

Laura plays basketball on the Red Racers team. How well did her team do? To find out, look at each scoreboard. Circle the team that won the game. On the back of the page, write a subtraction problem to show the difference in the score. Then write the correct answer on the line.

1

FINAL SCORE

Red Racers	93
Yellow Bees	68

The game was won

by _____ points.

2

FINAL SCORE

Silver Lightning	49
Red Racers	78

The game was won

by _____ points.

3

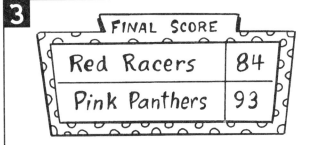

FINAL SCORE

Red Racers	84
Pink Panthers	93

The game was won

by _____ points.

4

FINAL SCORE

Blue Blizzard	106
Red Racers	114

The game was won

by _____ points.

5

FINAL SCORE

Red Racers	85
Orange Zippers	111

The game was won

by _____ points.

6

FINAL SCORE

Green Dragons	117
Red Racers	123

The game was won

by _____ points.

Name _____ Date _____

Movie Time

Look at how long each movie lasts. Subtract to find the difference between the length of the two movies. Write your answer in the box. Use the back of the page to show how you got your answers.

1

Spooky House	120 minutes
Crazy Cat	90 minutes

☐ minutes

2

Eggs-periment!	125 minutes
Two Goofy Guys	63 minutes

☐ minutes

3

The Voyage	175 minutes
Casey Takes Off	142 minutes

☐ minutes

4

Scary Story	160 minutes
Under the Sea	70 minutes

☐ minutes

5

The Last Octopus	162 minutes
Geno's Ghost	144 minutes

☐ minutes

6

The Old Owl Tree	135 minutes
Space Escape	127 minutes

☐ minutes

7

Noodlehead Tales	146 minutes
Star Battles	73 minutes

☐ minutes

8

Moo at the Zoo	185 minutes
Monkey Madness	78 minutes

☐ minutes

9

Moon Jumpers	138 minutes
The Race	56 minutes

☐ minutes

10

Galaxy Town	142 minutes
Jungle Mischief	85 minutes

☐ minutes

Practice, Practice, Practice! Addition & Subtraction Scholastic Teaching Resources

55

Name _____ Date _____

Wild Animal Shelter

The animal shelter takes care of hurt wild animals. Look at the chart to find out how many animals stayed at the shelter last year. Then use the information to answer the questions. Write a problem to show how you got each answer.

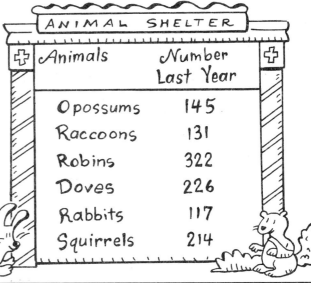

ANIMAL SHELTER	
Animals	Number Last Year
Opossums	145
Raccoons	131
Robins	322
Doves	226
Rabbits	117
Squirrels	214

1 How many more robins than raccoons were cared for at the shelter?

_____ robins

2 How many more squirrels than rabbits were cared for at the shelter?

_____ squirrels

3 How many more doves than opossums were cared for at the shelter?

_____ doves

4 How many more raccoons than rabbits were cared for at the shelter?

_____ raccoons

5 How many more robins than doves were cared for at the shelter?

_____ robins

6 How many more opossums than rabbits were cared for at the shelter?

_____ opossums

56

Facts Fountain

Start with 9 in the middle of the fountain.
Add or subtract the numbers along each stream.
Write your answers in the puddles. Then draw
an **X** on the puddle with the highest number.

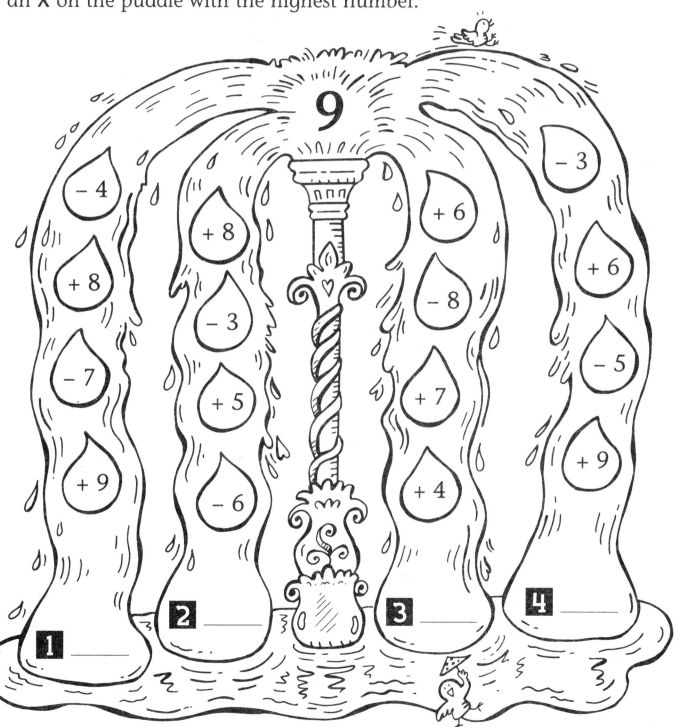

Number Families

Write all the equations that belong to each number family. The first one has been done for you. Hint: You can add or subtract in your equations.

1	5, 6, 11	2	9, 5, 14
	$5 + 6 = 11$ $11 - 6 = 5$		_____ _____
	$6 + 5 = 11$ $11 - 5 = 6$		_____ _____

3	7, 16, 9	4	12, 7, 5
	_____ _____		_____ _____
	_____ _____		_____ _____

5	5, 13, 8	6	15, 8, 7
	_____ _____		_____ _____
	_____ _____		_____ _____

Use a number less than 18 to fill in the missing number in each number family. On the back of the page, write all the equations that belong to each number family.

7	8, 14, _____	8	9, 17, _____

Practice, Practice, Practice! Addition & Subtraction Scholastic Teaching Resources

Nifty Nine Round-Ups

Here's a quick trick you can use when you add or subtract 9.

Addition	**Subtraction**

For the problem   36
            + 9
	For the problem 78
	            − 9

Round 9 up to 10.   36
            + 10
	Round 9 up to 10. 78
	            − 10

Solve your problem.   36
            + 10
            46
	Solve your problem. 78
	            − 10
	            68

Take away 1 from your answer. $46 - 1 = 45$	Add 1 to your answer. $68 + 1 = 69$
45 is the answer to your problem!	**69** is the answer to your problem!

Use the quick trick to complete the chains. Try to work out each answer in your head before your write it on the chain.

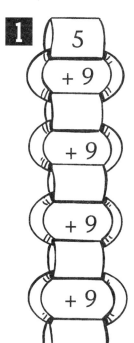

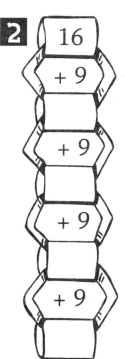

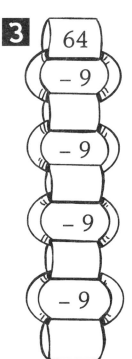

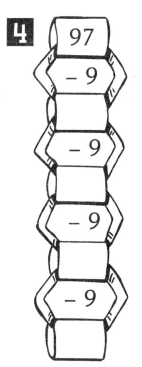

Practice, Practice, Practice! Addition & Subtraction   Scholastic Teaching Resources

59

Number Snakes

Start at each snake's head. Add or subtract the numbers along its body. Write your answer on the tail. Use the back of the page to show how you got your answers.

1

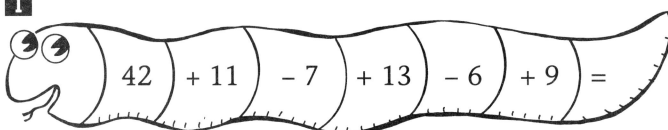

42 + 11 − 7 + 13 − 6 + 9 =

2

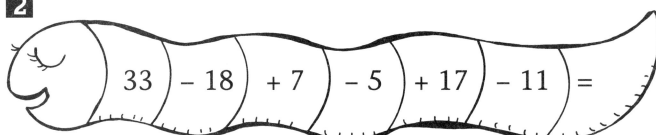

33 − 18 + 7 − 5 + 17 − 11 =

3

67 + 15 − 36 + 27 − 48 + 55 =

4

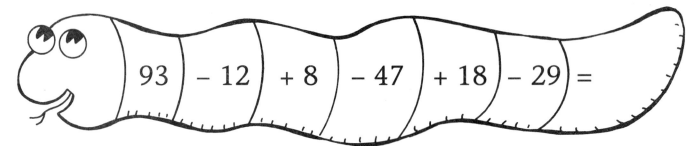

93 − 12 + 8 − 47 + 18 − 29 =

Practice, Practice, Practice! Addition & Subtraction   Scholastic Teaching Resources

Answer Key

Eight Chocolate Chips, page 7

The student should draw chocolate chips on the cookie pairs in any of the following combinations along with the corresponding equation:

0 and 8, 0 + 8 = 8;
1 and 7, 1 + 7 = 8;
2 and 6, 2 + 6 = 8;
3 and 5, 3 + 5 = 8;
4 and 4, 4 + 4 = 8;
5 and 3, 5 + 3 = 8;
6 and 2, 6 + 2 = 8;
7 and 1, 7 + 1 = 8;
8 and 0, 8 + 0 = 8

Underwater Addition, page 8

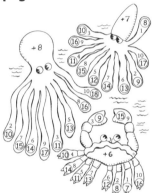

Taking Inventory, page 9

1. 7 + 5 = 12; 12
2. 9 + 6 = 15; 15
3. 7 + 6 = 13; 13
4. 7 + 9 = 16; 16
5. 6 + 8 = 14; 14
6. 10 + 10 = 20; 20
7. 9 + 8 = 17; 17
8. 4 + 7 = 11; 11

Puzzle Go-Togethers, page 10

A. 8 + 10 = 18
B. 5 + 6 = 11
C. 7 + 9 = 16
D. 6 + 13 = 19
E. 5 + 11 = 16
F. 4 + 9 = 13

Double Fun, page 11

1. 2; 1 + 1 = 2
2. 6; 3 + 3 = 6
3. 8; 4 + 4 = 8
4. 10; 5 + 5 = 10
5. 18; 9 + 9 = 18
6. 14; 7 + 7 = 14
7. 22; 11 + 11 = 22
8. 24; 12 + 12 = 24
9. The student should draw two faces, each with two eyes; 4 eyes
10. The student should draw two spiders, each with eight legs; 16 legs

The Pet Store, page 12

For each problem, the student should write the name of two animals that belong to the named category.

1. $12; $6 + $6 = $12
2. $16; $8 + $8 = $16
3. $18; $9 + $9 = $18
4. $14; $7 + $7 = $14

Number Juggle, page 13

1. 7 + 3 = 10
2. 6 + 7 = 13
3. 9 + 8 = 17
4. 8 + 4 = 12
5. 9 + 6 = 15
6. 11 + 2 = 13
7. 10 + 10 = 20
8. 8 + 5 = 13
9. 7 + 9 = 16
10. 2, 3, 4, 5, 6, 7, 8, 9, 10

Three-Penny Pitch, page 14

The student should write each addition problem on a sheet of paper. Problems and answers will vary.

Balloon Tic-Tac-Toe, page 15

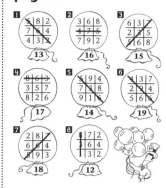

Billy's Baseball Caps, page 16

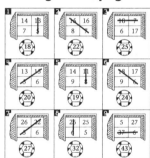

Scoring Goals, page 17

Little Pig's Problem, page 18

1. 47 + 6 = 53
2. 35 + 43 = 78
3. 28 + 14 = 42
4. 54 + 34 = 88
5. 85 + 6 = 91
6. 23 + 34 = 57
7. 13 + 76 = 89
8. 69 + 28 = 97
9. 52 + 26 = 78

Amazing Adding Machines, page 19

1. 30 + 10 = 40
2. 20 + 10 = 30
3. 50 + 10 = 60
4. 10 + 20 = 30
5. 50 + 20 = 70
6. 40 + 20 = 60
7. 20 + 30 = 50
8. 10 + 30 = 40
9. 60 + 30 = 90

Flower-Box Sums, page 20

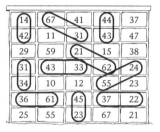

Easy-Add Estimates, page 21

1. 32 + 37 = 69; Estimate: 30 + 40 = 70
2. 27 + 61 = 88; Estimate: 30 + 60 = 90
3. 17 + 82 = 99; Estimate: 20 + 80 = 100
4. 36 + 21 = 57; Estimate: 40 + 20 = 60
5. 16 + 22 = 38; Estimate: 20 + 20 = 40
6. 43 + 36 = 79; Estimate: 40 + 40 = 80
7. 16 + 33 = 49; Estimate: 20 + 30 = 50
8. 21 + 12 = 33; Estimate: 20 + 10 = 30
9. 30, 40, 50, 60, 70, 80, 90, 100

Playful Pup, page 22

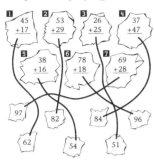

Animal Mail, page 23

1.   37 miles
     + 35 miles
       72 miles

2.   34 miles
     + 49 miles
       83 miles

3.   46 miles
     + 48 miles
       94 miles

4.   55 miles
     + 37 miles
       92 miles

5.   28 miles
     + 63 miles
       91 miles

Sum Challenge, page 24

The student should write one of these equations for the first part of the problem, and the other for the second part of the problem.

1. $85 + 76 = 161$;
   $86 + 75 = 161$
2. $58 + 67 = 125$;
   $57 + 68 = 125$
3. $96 + 87 = 183$;
   $97 + 86 = 183$
4. $69 + 78 = 147$;
   $68 + 79 = 147$

Silly Sal, page 25

1. 111; correct
2. 121; incorrect
3. 152; correct
4. 178; correct
5. 114; incorrect
6. 185; correct
7. 126; incorrect
8. 143; correct
9. 176; incorrect

On the Road, page 26

1.   322 km
       224 km
     + 211 km
       757 km

2.   211 km
       244 km
     + 130 km
       585 km

3.   231 km
       213 km
     + 322 km
       766 km

4.   130 km
       114 km
     + 153 km
       397 km

Balancing Animals, page 27

1. The student should glue the deer and penguin on the scale.
       206 lb.
     + 67 lb.
       273 lb.

2. The student should glue the leopard and snake on the scale.
       135 lb.
     + 55 lb.
       190 lb.

3. The student should glue the alligator and fox on the scale.
       356 lb.
     + 84 lb.
       440 lb.

Twins Buy Bikes, page 28

1. $57
     + $57
       $114

2. $76
     + $76
       $152

3. $69
     + $69
       $138

4. $196
     + $196
       $392

5. $158
     + $158
       $316

6. $367
     + $367
       $734

Big Creature Comparisons, page 29

1. Robotosaur   175 feet
       + 299 feet
         474 feet

2. Monsterdon   379 feet
       + 187 feet
         566 feet

3. Googlepup   133 feet
       + 235 feet
         368 feet

4. Googlepup   181 feet
       + 187 feet
         368 feet

5. Monsterdon   198 feet
       + 368 feet
         566 feet

6. Robotosaur   106 feet
       + 368 feet
         474 feet

Box of Chocolates, page 30

1. $10 - 3 = 7$; 7
2. $10 - 5 = 5$; 5
3. $10 - 8 = 2$; 2
4. $10 - 2 = 8$; 8
5. $10 - 4 = 6$; 6
6. $10 - 6 = 4$; 4
7. $10 - 7 = 3$; 3
8. $10 - 9 = 1$; 1
9. $10 - 1 = 9$; 9

Bobsled Race, pages 31–32

The student should give the correct answer for each of the ten game cards that he or she uses on the game board.

$5 - 3 = 2$	$14 - 5 = 9$
$6 - 4 = 2$	$12 - 4 = 8$
$9 - 3 = 6$	$13 - 6 = 7$
$16 - 7 = 9$	$13 - 8 = 5$
$11 - 5 = 6$	$10 - 3 = 7$
$8 - 4 = 4$	$15 - 7 = 8$
$17 - 8 = 9$	$10 - 7 = 3$
$7 - 3 = 4$	$11 - 7 = 4$
$9 - 5 = 4$	$14 - 8 = 6$
$9 - 7 = 2$	$11 - 6 = 5$
$12 - 5 = 7$	$10 - 6 = 4$
$18 - 9 = 9$	$15 - 9 = 6$
$8 - 3 = 5$	$14 - 7 = 7$
$14 - 9 = 5$	$12 - 6 = 6$
$8 - 5 = 3$	$17 - 9 = 8$
$13 - 9 = 4$	$16 - 8 = 8$
$15 - 6 = 9$	$10 - 5 = 5$
$7 - 2 = 5$	$14 - 6 = 8$
$11 - 4 = 7$	$12 - 7 = 5$
$8 - 6 = 2$	$9 - 8 = 1$

Free Mr. Fly, page 33

Animal Tracks, page 34

1. 15 cm $- 9$ cm $= 6$ cm;
   6 cm
2. 13 cm $- 6$ cm $= 7$ cm;
   7 cm
3. 17 cm $- 8$ cm $= 9$ cm;
   9 cm

Jungle Trail, page 35

13 − 6 = 7	18 − 9 = 9
14 − 5 = 9	12 − 4 = 8
14 − 7 = 7	13 − 4 = 9
15 − 8 = 7	6 − 4 = 2
9 − 4 = 5	10 − 5 = 5
11 − 7 = 4	10 − 6 = 4
14 − 6 = 8	7 − 3 = 4
9 − 5 = 4	8 − 3 = 5
13 − 9 = 4	12 − 3 = 9
15 − 6 = 9	16 − 9 = 7
9 − 3 = 6	8 − 4 = 4
14 − 8 = 6	10 − 2 = 8
12 − 7 = 5	10 − 4 = 6
17 − 9 = 8	13 − 7 = 6
15 − 9 = 6	13 − 9 = 4
12 − 5 = 7	11 − 5 = 6
16 − 3 = 13	15 − 5 = 10
12 − 6 = 6	10 − 3 = 7
8 − 5 = 3	15 − 7 = 8
14 − 9 = 5	17 − 8 = 9
16 − 7 = 9	9 − 7 = 2
16 − 8 = 8	12 − 9 = 3

Bug Olympics, page 36

1. 8 hours; 16 − 8 = 8
2. 5 hours; 12 − 7 = 5
3. caterpillar; 18 − 9 = 9
4. roly-poly; 16 − 4 = 12
5. 3 hours; 12 − 9 = 3
6. 11 hours; 18 − 7 = 11

People and Pets, page 37

1. 52 years
$$\begin{array}{r} 56 \\ -\ 4 \\ \hline 52 \end{array}$$

2. 25 years
$$\begin{array}{r} 28 \\ -\ 3 \\ \hline 25 \end{array}$$

3. 83 years
$$\begin{array}{r} 89 \\ -\ 6 \\ \hline 83 \end{array}$$

4. 72 years
$$\begin{array}{r} 74 \\ -\ 2 \\ \hline 72 \end{array}$$

5. 11 years
$$\begin{array}{r} 15 \\ -\ 4 \\ \hline 11 \end{array}$$

6. 44 years
$$\begin{array}{r} 47 \\ -\ 3 \\ \hline 44 \end{array}$$

7. 63 years
$$\begin{array}{r} 68 \\ -\ 5 \\ \hline 63 \end{array}$$

8. 21 years
$$\begin{array}{r} 29 \\ -\ 8 \\ \hline 21 \end{array}$$

Bunny Board Toss, pages 38–39

The student should write each subtraction problem on the score sheet. Problems and answers will vary.

Four From Three, page 40

1–4. Possible answers:

$$\begin{array}{r} 23 \\ -\ 5 \\ \hline 18 \end{array} \quad \begin{array}{r} 32 \\ -\ 5 \\ \hline 27 \end{array} \quad \begin{array}{r} 52 \\ -\ 3 \\ \hline 49 \end{array}$$

$$\begin{array}{r} 25 \\ -\ 3 \\ \hline 22 \end{array} \quad \begin{array}{r} 35 \\ -\ 2 \\ \hline 33 \end{array} \quad \begin{array}{r} 53 \\ -\ 2 \\ \hline 51 \end{array}$$

5–8. Possible answers:

$$\begin{array}{r} 45 \\ -\ 6 \\ \hline 39 \end{array} \quad \begin{array}{r} 54 \\ -\ 6 \\ \hline 48 \end{array} \quad \begin{array}{r} 64 \\ -\ 5 \\ \hline 59 \end{array}$$

$$\begin{array}{r} 46 \\ -\ 5 \\ \hline 41 \end{array} \quad \begin{array}{r} 56 \\ -\ 4 \\ \hline 52 \end{array} \quad \begin{array}{r} 65 \\ -\ 4 \\ \hline 61 \end{array}$$

Giant-Size Subtraction, page 41

1. 223 cm
$$\begin{array}{r} 232 \text{ cm} \\ -\ 9 \text{ cm} \\ \hline 223 \text{ cm} \end{array}$$

2. 147 cm
$$\begin{array}{r} 153 \text{ cm} \\ -\ 6 \text{ cm} \\ \hline 147 \text{ cm} \end{array}$$

3. 183 cm
$$\begin{array}{r} 191 \text{ cm} \\ -\ 8 \text{ cm} \\ \hline 183 \text{ cm} \end{array}$$

4. 127 cm
$$\begin{array}{r} 134 \text{ cm} \\ -\ 7 \text{ cm} \\ \hline 127 \text{ cm} \end{array}$$

5. 239 cm
$$\begin{array}{r} 248 \text{ cm} \\ -\ 9 \text{ cm} \\ \hline 239 \text{ cm} \end{array}$$

6. 379 cm
$$\begin{array}{r} 386 \text{ cm} \\ -\ 7 \text{ cm} \\ \hline 379 \text{ cm} \end{array}$$

Challenge!, pages 42–43

Answers will vary.

Space Subtraction, page 44

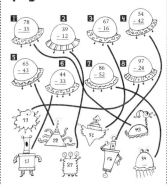

Subtraction Shape Sentences, page 45

1. 86 − 32 = 54
2. 47 − 24 = 23
3. 99 − 63 = 36
4. 25 − 15 = 10
5. 68 − 43 = 25
6. 85 − 22 = 63
7. 79 − 31 = 48

How Late Is Sam?, page 46

1. 12 minutes
$$\begin{array}{r} 42 \\ -\ 30 \\ \hline 12 \end{array}$$

2. 32 minutes
$$\begin{array}{r} 57 \\ -\ 25 \\ \hline 32 \end{array}$$

3. 13 minutes
$$\begin{array}{r} 28 \\ -\ 15 \\ \hline 13 \end{array}$$

4. 11 minutes
$$\begin{array}{r} 56 \\ -\ 45 \\ \hline 11 \end{array}$$

5. 23 minutes
$$\begin{array}{r} 49 \\ -\ 26 \\ \hline 23 \end{array}$$

6. 23 minutes
$$\begin{array}{r} 58 \\ -\ 35 \\ \hline 23 \end{array}$$

The Pond Store, page 47

1. 44¢
$$\begin{array}{r} 68¢ \\ -24¢ \\ \hline 44¢ \end{array}$$
33¢
$$\begin{array}{r} 68¢ \\ -35¢ \\ \hline 33¢ \end{array}$$
43¢
$$\begin{array}{r} 68¢ \\ -25¢ \\ \hline 43¢ \end{array}$$

2. 76¢
$$\begin{array}{r} 89¢ \\ -13¢ \\ \hline 76¢ \end{array}$$
77¢
$$\begin{array}{r} 89¢ \\ -12¢ \\ \hline 77¢ \end{array}$$
47¢
$$\begin{array}{r} 89¢ \\ -42¢ \\ \hline 47¢ \end{array}$$

3. 11¢
$$\begin{array}{r} 46¢ \\ -35¢ \\ \hline 11¢ \end{array}$$
33¢
$$\begin{array}{r} 46¢ \\ -13¢ \\ \hline 33¢ \end{array}$$
24¢
$$\begin{array}{r} 46¢ \\ -22¢ \\ \hline 24¢ \end{array}$$

4. 45¢
$$\begin{array}{r} 57¢ \\ -12¢ \\ \hline 45¢ \end{array}$$
35¢
$$\begin{array}{r} 57¢ \\ -22¢ \\ \hline 35¢ \end{array}$$
46¢
$$\begin{array}{r} 57¢ \\ -11¢ \\ \hline 46¢ \end{array}$$

Butterfly Differences, page 48

1. 39; The student should color the wings yellow.

2. 25; The student should color the wings blue.

3. Top: 24; The student should color the top wings white.

   Bottom: 26; The student should color the bottom wings orange.

4. 58; The student should color the wings purple.

5. Top: 58; The student should color the top wings purple.

   Bottom: 26; The student should color the bottom wings orange.

6. Top: 26; The student should color the top wings orange.

   Bottom: 39; The student should color the bottom wings yellow.

Checking Chuck, page 49

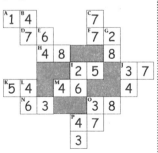

Number Connection, page 50

Number Connection Clues, page 51

Across	Down
A. 14	B. 47
D. 76	C. 77
F. 72	E. 64
H. 48	G. 28
I. 25	I. 26
J. 37	J. 34
K. 54	L. 46
M. 46	O. 37
N. 63	P. 43
O. 38	
P. 47	

Magazine Subtraction, page 52

Answers will vary.

Collection Kids, page 53

1. 200 bottle caps
2. 300 ants
3. 500 baseball cards
4. 700 paper clips
5. 300 stamps
6. 400 marbles
7. 400 stickers
8. 400 pennies

Basketball Scores, page 54

1. The student should circle Red Racers; 25

   $$93 - 68 = 25$$

2. The student should circle Red Racers; 29

   $$78 - 49 = 29$$

3. The student should circle Pink Panthers; 9

   $$93 - 84 = 9$$

4. The student should circle Red Racers; 8

   $$114 - 106 = 8$$

5. The student should circle Orange Zippers; 26

   $$111 - 85 = 26$$

6. The student should circle Red Racers; 6

   $$123 - 117 = 6$$

Movie Time, page 55

1. 30 minutes
2. 62 minutes
3. 33 minutes
4. 90 minutes
5. 18 minutes
6. 8 minutes
7. 73 minutes
8. 107 minutes
9. 82 minutes
10. 57 minutes

Wild Animal Shelter, page 56

1. 191 $$322 - 131 = 191$$

2. 97 $$214 - 117 = 97$$

3. 81 $$226 - 145 = 81$$

4. 14 $$131 - 117 = 14$$

5. 96 $$322 - 226 = 96$$

6. 28 $$145 - 117 = 28$$

Facts Fountain, page 57

1. 15
2. 13
3. 18
4. 16

The student should draw an X on 3.

Number Families, page 58

1. 5 + 6 = 11; 6 + 5 = 11; 11 − 6 = 5; 11 − 5 = 6

2. 9 + 5 = 14; 5 + 9 = 14; 14 − 9 = 5; 14 − 5 = 9

3. 7 + 9 = 16; 9 + 7 = 16; 16 − 7 = 9; 16 − 9 = 7

4. 7 + 5 = 12; 5 + 7 = 12; 12 − 5 = 7; 12 − 7 = 5

5. 5 + 8 = 13; 8 + 5 = 13; 13 − 8 = 5; 13 − 5 = 8

6. 7 + 8 = 15; 8 + 7 = 15; 15 − 8 = 7; 15 − 7 = 8

7. 6 + 8 = 14; 8 + 6 = 14; 14 − 6 = 8; 14 − 8 = 6

8. 9 + 8 = 17; 8 + 9 = 17; 17 − 8 = 9; 17 − 9 = 8

Nifty Nine Round-Ups, page 59

1. 14, 23, 32, 41
2. 25, 34, 43, 52
3. 55, 46, 37, 28
4. 88, 79, 70, 61

Number Snakes, page 60

1. 62
2. 23
3. 80
4. 31